P9-DME-927

Little Grover's Book of Shapes

Featuring Jim Henson's Sesame Street Muppets

By Anna Ross • Illustrated by Norman Gorbaty

Random House / Children's Television Workshop

Library of Congress Cataloging-in-Publication Data
Ross, Anna. Little Grover's book of shapes / by Anna Ross ; illustrated by Norman Gorbaty. p. cm. – (A Sesame Street toddler book)
Summary: Little Grover discovers various shapes in the objects around him, including squares, triangles, and stars.
ISBN 0-679-82237-2 1. Geometry–Juvenile literature. [1. Shape.] I. Gorbaty, Norman, ill. II. Title. III. Series. QA445.5.R66 1992
516.2–dc20 91-4920

Manufactured in Italy 10 9 8 7 6 5 4 3 2 1

Little Grover, what is round?

This pie, this cookie,
and this shiny white plate.
The wheels on my
brand-new roller skate.

Little Grover, what is a square?

Herry's game board
and Big Bird's box,
Elmo's dollhouse
and Betty Lou's blocks.

Little Grover, what is a triangle?

That sail on the boat,
this flag in the air,
the pirate's hat,
a sandwich to share.

Little Grover, what is a rectangle?

Ernie's paper
and Big Bird's book,
my new camera
and the picture I took.

Little Grover, what is an oval?

Big Bird's mirror
and Oscar's grapes,
and eggs are perfect
oval shapes.

Little Grover, what is a diamond?

Kites, the pattern
on Bert's socks and shirt,
the shape that Ernie
drew in the dirt.

Little Grover, what is a cone?

Herry's ice cream cone,
my crayon tip,
Bert's paper cup,
and Elmo's rocket ship.

Little Grover, what is a star?

Stars are my favorite shape of all.
I have them on my jammies,
and I have them on my ball.
I have them on my pillow and—oh my!
Look out my window.
They are twinkling in the sky!

Look around in the world.
There are shapes all over!

Thank you for showing us shapes,
Little Grover!